D0346048

This boo

First published in paperback in 2003
Published by
Evans Brothers Limited
2A Portman Mansions
Chiltern Street
London W1U 6NR

First published 1999
Reprinted 2001, 2003
© in the text Keith Good 1999
© in the illustrations Evans Brothers Limited 1999

Series editor: Su Swallow
Illustrations and page design: Tim Scrivens, T J Graphics
Production: Jenny Mulvanny

Printed in Hong Kong by Wing King Tong Co. Ltd

Good, Keith
Moulding materials. – (Design challenge)
1. Materials – Juvenile Literature
I. Title II. Scrivens, Tim
620.1'1

ISBN 0 237 52541 0

For details of initial teacher training and in-service courses in
Design Technology at the University of Greenwich, contact
Keith Good by fax +44 (0)208 331 9504 or e-mail
k.w.good@gre.ac.uk

NORFOLK	
LIBRARIES & INFORMATION SERVICE	
429879	
PETERS	15-Jul-04
620.11	£6.99

Acknowledgments

For permission to reproduce copyright material the authors
and publishers gratefully acknowledge the following:

page 10 Michael Rosenfeld, Tony Stone Images **page 12**
Alan Abamowitz, Tony Stone Images**page 10** Last Resort
Picture Library **page 18** Last Resort Picture Library
page 20 Mike Timo, Tony Stone Worldwide **page 22** Last
Resort Picture Library **page 26** John Kelly, Tony Stone
Worldwide

DESIGN CHALLENGE

Moulding Materials

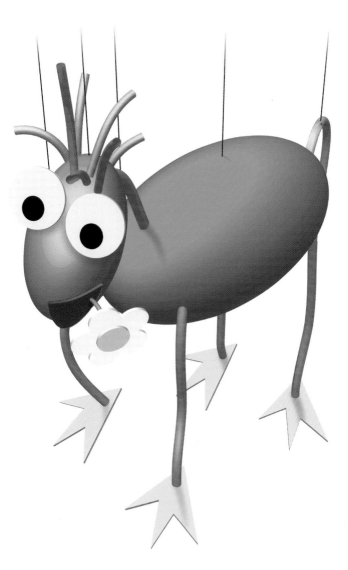

Keith Good

Evans

About this book

About this series

This series involves children in *designing* and making their own working technology projects, using readily available salvaged or cheap materials. Each project is based on a 'recipe' that promotes success and crucially, stimulates the reader's own ideas. The 'recipes' also provide a good introduction to important technology in everyday life. The projects can be developed to different levels of sophistication according to the reader's ability and can reflect their other interests. The series teaches skills and knowledge in a fun way and encourages creative, innovative ideas.

About this book

One reason for children to work with mouldable materials is that they are a major part of their environment. Children are literally surrounded by mouldable materials as they live and work in brick and concrete homes and classrooms. They sit on moulded chairs, cross moulded bridges, make moulded sandcastles and eat moulded bread, jellies, lollipops and biscuits. The many plastic products that children use such as toys and computer keyboards are also moulded. Not all mouldable materials are suitable for children but the ones in this book can be shaped quickly and easily so that plenty of ideas can be explored even when time is limited. Little equipment is needed. Fingers are often the best tools of all, giving real hands-on experience. Some processes like stamping (page 14) lend themselves to mass production, allowing this important concept to be discussed. Hollow forms (page 20) are among project parts that would be very difficult to make using other methods and materials. Scientific ideas about the way materials behave (changing when heated for example) can be brought to life through project work. Mouldable materials are among the first that children use. Through this book they can explore a range of materials and important processes and apply them creatively with increasing sophistication.

Safety

● Sharp tools are not necessary but any that are chosen should be used under supervision.

● Using ovens needs adult supervision and thick oven gloves. Do not overheat plastic sheets.

● Do not use wallpaper paste containing fungicide to make papier mâché.

● Check that thread used to hold decorations round any part of the body breaks easily if snagged.

● Containers to be examined as part of designing moulded containers should be well washed out before children handle them.

● Ensure that good hygiene is observed when making food projects.

Contents

Materials that can be moulded play an important part in the world around us. They are very easy to shape into the things we need. When moulds are used, many things such as house bricks, clay pots and plastic toys can be copied quickly and cheaply. When shapes are moulded, nothing is wasted by cutting away unwanted parts. Plasticine stays soft and can be moulded over and over again. Other materials like concrete and plaster set hard when they are dry. Materials like clay are natural and very long-lasting – we can still see the footprints of dinosaurs where they moulded clay by treading in it!

You will need

- things moulded from different materials
- pictures of moulded things
- coloured paper, pens and other things for making a display

What to do

1. Set up display area for a display about mouldable materials. Use a table or other surface for standing things on and a wall or pinboard for pictures.

2. Cover your display area with cloth or coloured paper so that your display will look good and things can be seen clearly.

3. Make your display as interesting and attractive as you can.

Mouldable materials can be shaped by hand (page 12), stamped (page 14), extruded (page 16) and cast (page 18).

Getting ideas

When setting up your display, think of ways to show the different kinds of mouldable materials and what they are used for. Try to show how important they are and give samples for your audience to handle. Look at how displays are done in your school, in shops and other places. Museums are a really good place to see how things can be displayed. What makes a good display? Some displays get people to do things as well as just look. Do activities help people to understand and make a display more fun? Could you design display activities?

You could use a computer to find and print information, instructions and labels.

Making mouldable materials

From plaster to papier mâché

Lots of materials can be moulded but some need special equipment, others are unsafe or expensive. Here are some materials you can use. Look out for these materials in use around you. Leave projects that need to dry in a warm place so that they will be ready quicker. Always protect your working area with a plastic sheet and wear an apron to protect your clothes.

You will need

To try out some of the projects in this book you will need:
- plain flour
- salt
- water
- air-drying clay
- plaster
- sandpaper
- Mod-roc
- newspaper
- tissue paper
- foam plastic sheet (such as Plastazote or Formafoam)

Salt dough

1. Mix 2 measures of plain flour and 1 measure of salt. Gradually add 1 measure of water. Knead (squeeze, mix and squash) the dough until it moulds well.

2. When you have made your project, put it on a baking tray in an oven to harden. **Safety:** Get adult help when using the oven. Cook at a low heat (about 100° Centigrade, gas mark 1/4). A long time on a low heat is best. Big or thick pieces will take longest.

3. Wire hooks and other things can be moulded into the dough before baking. 4. Leave your project to cool before painting.

Air-drying clay

1. Mould the clay to the shape you want using fingers, plastic picnic knives and forks and other things like old pen caps that you can find. Beads can be made by moulding round a rod.

2. Leave to dry well. Keep unused clay well wrapped in plastic to stop it going hard.

Normal clay has to be *fired* (baked) in an oven. Bricks and tiles are made this way.

Plaster

1. Mix 3 measures of plaster with 1 of water. Stir well. Tap the mould gently as you pour in the liquid.

2. Take out of the mould when dry. Smooth sharp edges with sandpaper. Paint when very dry. Wire, hooks and other things can be embedded in the plaster before it sets.

This process is called *casting* (see page 18). Plaster casts are used to decorate walls and ceilings and to make lasting copies of animal tracks and footprints.

Foam plastic sheet

Only use special foam sold for moulding and modelling. Brand names include Plastazote and Formafoam.

1. **Safety**: Get adult help to warm the sheet in an electric oven set to 150°C. A 6mm thick sheet will need to be warmed for about one minute. Smelly or sticky sheet is too hot.

2. Use oven gloves to take the sheet out of the oven. When it has cooled a little but is still warm, mould it to the shape you want. For example, a warm strip can be wound round a pencil to make a spiral.

3. Sheets can also be cut with scissors, sewn, stapled and glued. Plastic foam is used for gym mats, shoe liners, and swimming pool floats. (This kind of foam is NOT suitable for projects in this book.) Look out for other uses.

Mod-roc

This is a special cloth with plaster which you drape over a *former* (like Plasticine or a plastic bottle). It is like the plaster used to hold broken limbs still while they get better.

1. Wipe the former with petroleum jelly.

2. Take enough Mod-roc to cover the former twice and cut it into squares.

3. Dip each square into tepid water for four or five seconds. When the bubbles stop, squeeze the Mod-roc gently and smooth it over the former to dry.

Papier mâché

1. Tear pieces of newspaper into strips.

2. Make a paste by adding water to flour a little at a time.

3. Put the strips on a tray and brush them with the paste.

4. Drape the pasted strips over a former to make the shape you want. Use tissue paper for the last layer to make a smooth surface.

Balloons and bottles can be used as formers. Strips can also be pressed into a mould (such as a dish).

5. Leave to dry well before painting.

Papier mâché is French for 'chewed newspaper'. It has been used to make furniture, trays, bowls and other household items.

M--ul --l-m teri l- t-- e t

Basic recipes for biscuits and bread

Safety

Food safety and hygiene is important!

Tie back long hair and wear a clean apron.

Wash hands with soap, dry with a clean towel.

All equipment must be clean and only used for food. Wash after use and dry with a clean cloth.

Work on a clean surface.

Don't cough or sneeze over food or equipment.

Remember that some people must not eat certain foods.

Get adult help with food safety and using an oven.

You will need

Basic biscuit recipe
- 125g soft margarine
- 125g brown or white sugar
- 250g plain flour
- 1 egg
- pinch of salt

Biscuit recipe

1. Beat the margarine and sugar together in a bowl.

2. Beat the egg and add it to the mixture.

3. Add the flour and salt and mix to make dough.

4. Roll out the dough and cut or stamp out the shapes you want.

5. Put the shapes on a greased baking tray and cook in a medium hot oven (about 190°C or gas mark 5) for about 15 minutes.

You will need

Basic bread recipe
- 500g of flour
- 250ml of warm water
- 1 level teaspoon of salt
- 2 tablespoons of sunflower oil
- 1 sachet of dried yeast

Bread recipe

1. Mix the ingredients in a large bowl.

2. Mix spices well in if these are wanted (divide the mix if you want to try different ones).

3. Knead the dough.

4. Leave the dough to rise for at least 20 minutes.

5. Put on a baking tray and place in an oven set to 225°C, gas mark 8, for 15-20 minutes.

Drawing
Modelling your ideas on paper

Drawings are an important way of giving information. Instruction books, car repair manuals, dressmaking patterns and all sorts of plans are used every day. They give information quickly and can be understood by people who don't speak the same language. Drawings are also a good way for people to explore their own ideas. Drawing helps you to think things through – keeping all your ideas in your head is difficult! Although moulded materials are quick to shape, drawing can be an even quicker way to try out ideas. Drawing also helps you to talk to others about your ideas and gives you a record of the thinking that led to your final design.

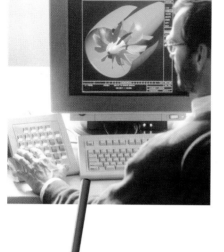

You will need

- A4 paper
- drawing and colouring equipment

Tip

Keep your eyes on the cross. Don't stare at the pencil point.

Concentrate on the last line you did.

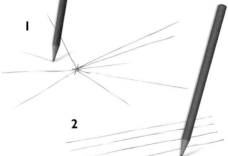

1

2

What to do

1. Draw a small cross and practise drawing lines to it. Start close to the cross and then gradually draw from further away.

2. Draw a line and practise drawing lines parallel to it. Start with lines close together and gradually draw them further apart.

3. Fix your paper over the square grid on page 28 with paperclips. Use paper that allows the grid to show through. Paper used for photocopying is good for this. Draw faint frames to help you draw lots of squares and circles. Next, try designing interesting counters for a board game. The *centre line (C/L)* is important when the object is *symmetrical* (both halves are the same).

You can use the square grid to help you draw projects. To help you cut out the clay or dough to the right shape, trace your drawing to make a *pattern* or *template*.

C/L

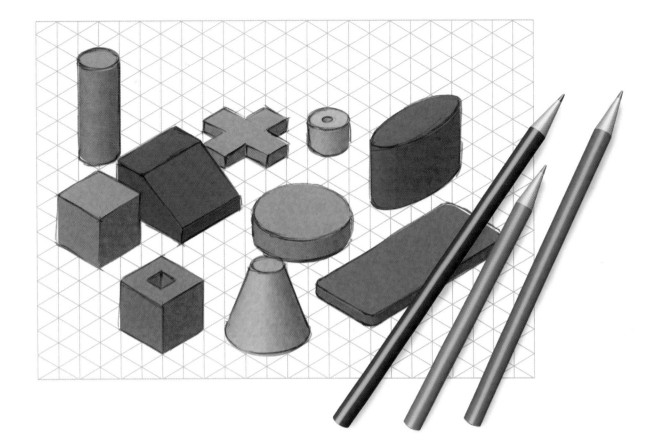

4. Fix your paper over the *isometric* grid on page 29 and practise drawing the shapes shown above. Draw faint frames to help you.

Many things you need to draw can be made up of simple shapes like these.

5. Using the same grid, make a drawing of the shapes assembled to make an interesting object. You could design a product of the future or one of the other projects in this book.

6. Lots of mouldable materials projects have rounded edges and corners. Practise by drawing shapes faintly with sharp edges, then round them off.

7. You can make your drawings look more real by shading them to show the light and dark surfaces. Top surfaces are often the lightest. If you are using coloured pencils use darker and lighter shades.

You can also use lines, dots and perhaps colour to show what something is made from.

M--ulding by han

Pots, cord pulls and zip pulls

Hard materials can only be shaped with a tool. Mouldable materials are soft enough to be shaped just with hands. Potters and sculptors often shape clay with their hands. Cooks mould food by hand. Many things we use need to be shaped so that they fit our hands well. Squeezing Plasticine is one way to find a good shape for a handle, which can then be copied in a harder material. You can shape air-drying clay and salt dough just using your hands. When these materials go hard the things you make can do useful jobs. Try the cord and zip pull activity on the next page, but first explore what your hands can do with mouldable materials.

You will need

- Plasticine
- salt dough (see page 7)
- air-drying clay (see page 7)
- white glue
- thin garden wire
- paints

What to do

1. Take some Plasticine and notice how it feels and behaves when you squeeze it, stretch it, twist it and press it.

2. Try to make a small thumb pot. Can you make a shape that will float?

3. Roll the Plasticine, twist and coil it.

Have you made any shapes that could be used for something – especially if they were made in a material that set hard?

Reinforced concrete has steel rods inside to add strength. Shaping the dough or clay round wire will make your moulding stronger, especially where it is quite narrow.

When dough and clay are hard they are quite brittle so don't make shapes that are very thin or narrow. Wire is also useful when you want to join something to your moulding.

reinforced concrete with steel rods

steel rod

What to do

1. Read 'Getting ideas' below and think about what your project will be for and what it will be like. Draw some different ideas.

2. For a cord pull, mould round a rod so that there will be a hole for the cord. For a zip pull, make a wire shape. A bent shape will grip the dough or clay better than a straight one.

3. Mould the shape you want. Leave air-drying clay to dry and harden. With adult help, bake a salt dough project and let it cool.

4. Paint your project and leave it to dry. Varnish with watered-down white glue, which will dry clear.

You could tie your project to a zip pull, but a small metal split ring is a neater way to join the two together. Get an adult to help you fix the ring. Tie a knot in the cord to keep a cord pull in place.

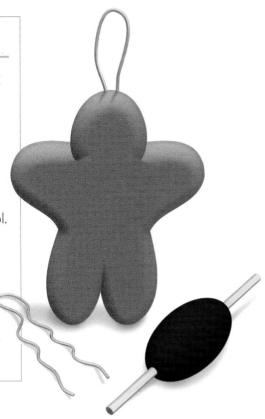

Getting ideas

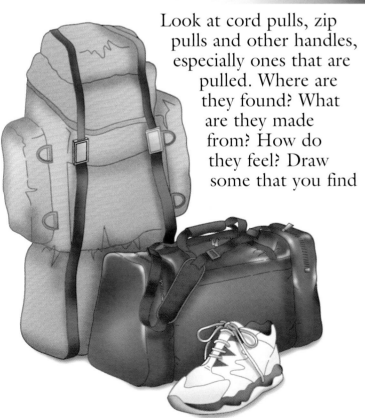

Look at cord pulls, zip pulls and other handles, especially ones that are pulled. Where are they found? What are they made from? How do they feel? Draw some that you find and make notes about them. What do you like and dislike? How could you improve them?

Play with a piece of dough to find out what shapes can be made. What patterns and textures can be made by pressing things into the dough? Remember to avoid thin shapes that might break.

As well as looking good your pull will need to fit the fingers or hand. Think about how it will be used. Will the user be wearing gloves? Where will your pull be used? Consider sports bags, clothing, roller blinds, light switches and other ideas.

Rolling, stamping and marking
Making shapes and decorating them

Rolling is used to shape metal and other materials. The hot metal is squeezed between sets of rollers which are closer and closer together until the metal is the right thickness. Rolling pins are used in kitchens to roll pastry into thin sheets. Clay and other mouldable materials can also be rolled. *Stamping* is a quick way of cutting out shapes from flat sheets. Coins, biscuits, milk bottle caps and other things are stamped out in large numbers. Cooks use cutters to cut out shapes from pastry. Stamping or pressing into material is a good way to decorate surfaces and lots of marks can be made the same. You can roll, stamp and mark to make puzzles, games and parts for other projects like the one on page 19.

You will need

- Plasticine (for trying out your ideas first)
- air-drying clay
- two strips of wood
- rolling pin kept for clay work, or short piece of broom handle
- interesting things to use for stamping and marking

What to do

1. On a smooth board, roll out a slab of clay large enough for your project. Using two strips of wood will give you an even thickness. Thin strips can be taped together if a thicker slab is needed.

2. A paper template will help if you want to cut out shapes that are the same. Fold and cut out a template if you want to make symmetrical shapes (one with both halves the same shape).

3. Use a modelling tool or plastic knife to cut round your template. You can also cut out pieces by measuring and marking on the slab. Use a wet finger to make any rounded edges that you want.

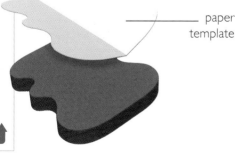

paper template

4. Unwanted pastry and biscuit cutters are good for stamping out shapes. You can use glue stick caps and other lids to stamp out parts for projects. It is easier to get the disks out when you use a tube that is open at both ends.

5. Find things to press into the clay to mark the surface of things like games playing pieces, decorative tiles and other things.

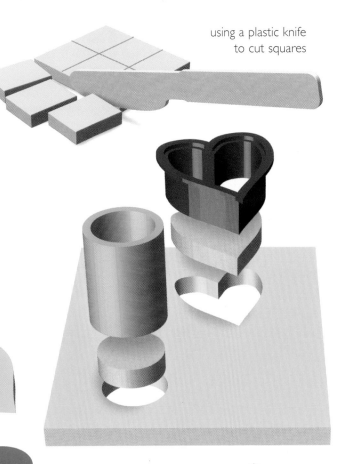

using a plastic knife to cut squares

Tip
Brush shapes with water to stick them to other pieces of clay.

Getting ideas

You could design jigsaw puzzles by rolling, stamping out and marking a design or picture, then cutting it into pieces. Parts could be made to fit together. You could try out your design in card or Plasticine first. Don't make it too easy or too hard. You could design games that use playing pieces that have been stamped out and marked. The playing board could be made in card or even in fabric. You could design your own dice. You could use a computer to write rules and to make numbers and shapes for your games board. If you don't have a colour printer you could colour a black and white printout. Could you design a game that could also be played by people with sight problems or with eyes covered? Which are easiest to feel – pieces stuck on or marks pressed into the surface? Finding out about games from different countries could help you have your own ideas.

Extruding mouldable materials

Making a minibeast

Extruding is a way of shaping material by pushing it through a hole so that it comes out the same shape as the hole. Toothpaste coming out of a tube is being extruded. Cakes are decorated by squeezing icing through a shaped nozzle. Some biscuits and other foods are extruded. When they are hot enough, metals like aluminium are soft enough to be extruded to make window frames and other things. Plastic pipes, insulation on electric wires and other everyday products are also made by extrusion. You can extrude materials like salt dough, air-drying clay and Plasticine by pushing them through sieves, graters and other things with holes in them. One use for the shapes is to make new creatures or minibeasts that you have designed.

You will need

- Plasticine
- salt dough or air-drying clay
- an unwanted tea strainer, sieve and other things with holes to try
- nail brush

What to do

1. Try out extruding by pushing some Plasticine through a sieve or tea strainer. This will make shapes that look like hair or fur that can be scraped off using a plastic knife.

2. Salt dough and air-drying clay can also be pushed through holes to make lasting projects. Experiment with other tools such as a garlic press.

3. Different amounts of water in the dough or clay will change how it behaves. You could divide your clay or dough into same-sized pieces and add a different number of drops of water to each. Add a few drops of water at a time and work it in well before deciding whether to add more.

Quite wet clay pushes straight through a grater well but when you want to take shavings off a block, is a drier block better?

A toy 'dough factory' will extrude lots of different shapes if your material is soft enough. Wash it well before the clay or dough dries.

Creating a creature

1. Use books and CD ROMs to find out about small creatures. Use the ideas on this page to help you design a new creature.

2. You can use extruding with processes like hand-moulding (see page 12), rolling, stamping and marking (see page 14).

3. Thin parts made from clay or dough would be very fragile so mould in wire to make parts like legs and feelers. Thin parts of a body can also be made stronger with wire.

4. Add any extruded or stamped out parts. Brush with water to help pieces stick. You could mark the surface with cocktail sticks and other tools.

5. Get adult help to bake a salt dough creature (see page 7) and let it cool. Leave an air-drying clay creature to dry well. Paint carefully, then stick on parts if you wish.

Getting ideas

To help you get ideas for your new creature or minibeast, take a close look at pictures of real ones.

What do they look like? How do they protect themselves? What do they eat and how do they find their food? How will *your* minibeast live? What will it eat? Are there animals that hunt your creature? Does it hunt other creatures, live on plants, candle wax or even litter? Find out about *food chains* in nature. What senses will your creature have? How will it find or catch its food? How will it protect itself? How will it move?

What will your minibeast be called? Could it be a robot bug? It could have an everyday name, a scientific name and a pet name. Design a care manual to tell people about your creature and how to look after it. Use a computer to do this if you can.

Casting
Making models with moulds

Pouring molten metal, liquid plaster, wet concrete, jelly or some other material into a mould is called *casting*. When the material sets or cools, it hardens and becomes the same shape as the mould. Casting is a quick way of making copies of something, and very little material is wasted. Candles, ice cubes, paving stones and parts for buildings and bridges are all made by casting. You can design your own electronic product using casting. Many of the electronic objects around us started as models. Designers use non-working models to try out their new ideas and show them to others. Your product does not really have to work so use your imagination!

You will need

- plaster
- water
- moulded plastic packaging or clear plastic bubble pack
- Plasticine

Tip

Two castings from the same mould can be glued together. Smooth the back of the castings on sandpaper.

What to do

1. Find some packaging to use as a mould. Choose one that is the right shape for your design ideas. Use Plasticine to hold the mould level if you need to.

2. Mix up the plaster (see page 7) and pour it into the mould, tapping the mould to help it flow. Leave to set, then take the casting out.

3. When the casting is really dry, use sandpaper to take off any sharp edges. The project can now be painted. Stickers and parts that you find can be stuck on to make controls, screens and other things.

What to do

Here is how to make another kind of mould:

1. Make a slab of Plasticine (see page 14) on a board. Press a strip of Plasticine firmly around the edge of the slab to make the wall of the mould.

2. Use modelling tools and other things to press in and shape the mould. You can also add Plasticine shapes.

Remember that you are working in reverse. Make a dent in the Plasticine and it will come out as a bump on your cast. Add a raised shape to the slab and it will come out as a dip.

3. Pour in the plaster and leave it to set.

4. Take the plaster cast out of the mould and paint it. When dry, varnish with watered down white glue.

Tip

Put your mould (on its board) in a large bowl or a tray in case it leaks.

Getting ideas

Think about designing and modelling an electronic project of the future. Electronic products are a very important part of the world around us. How many could you list? Imagine if there were no calculators, computer games, pagers, hand-held computers or mobile phones. Look at products that already exist in your home, school, shops and catalogues. How could they be improved? What extra things could they do? What new products would *you* like to have? What will people really need in the future? What would the *real* version of your product do? Ask other people for their ideas. A busy parent might like a device that stopped a toddler wandering off (it would need to be safe and kind to the child!). Think about what controls you would need and where they should be put. Think about colour, shape, size, good looks and safety. Write and draw a user's manual or instruction leaflet for your product. For a very realistic manual, use a computer (word-processing, desktop publishing, graphics, colour printing).

Hollow moulding

Making puppets for a play

Hollow mouldings weigh very little for their size because they are full of air! Large things can be made without using much material because the mouldings are hollow. Plastic footballs, dolls and bottles are all hollow mouldings. Some are made by blowing softened plastic into a mould. Other things, such as canoes, are made by joining two mouldings together. You can make hollow mouldings using papier mâché or Mod-roc (see page 8). You could make some shapes in each material to compare them. The spaces inside could be used to hold things like batteries, wires, bulbs and other working parts. You could use a hollow moulding when designing a puppet!

You will need

- papier mâché or Mod-roc (see page 8)
- Plasticine
- petroleum jelly
- balloons

1

2

3

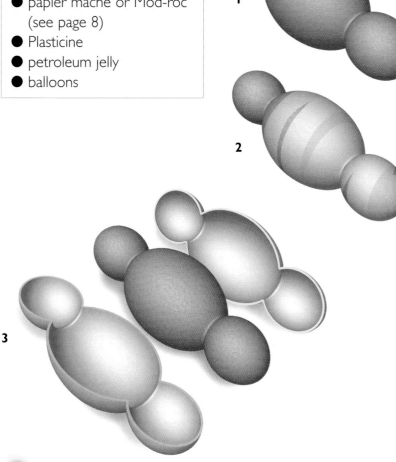

What to do

1. Decide what shape you want your puppet to be and mould the shape in Plasticine. Wipe it over with petroleum jelly. This will stop the covering sticking to it.

2. Choose your covering – papier mâché or Mod-roc. Smooth several layers over the Plasticine. Put in a warm place to dry well.

3. Get adult help to cut the moulding in half and take out the Plasticine. This would be a good time to make holes ready for tying on things like legs, neck and control strings (see page 21).

4. Use strips of the covering to join the halves together again.

What to do

Here's how to make bigger hollow mouldings:

1. Blow up a balloon and build several layers of covering over it.

2. When the covering is dry, push a pin in to pop the balloon!

3. To fix strings on, tie the end to a used match or small piece of stick and thread it into the hole.

Tip

You could use a balloon to make the largest part of your puppet and Plasticine formers to make a head and other smaller parts.

Getting ideas

There are many kinds of puppet. What will your puppet be like? What sort of character will it be? It could just hang from one string or piece of elastic or have several moving parts. You could get together with friends and write a play. Perhaps your puppet or play could be used to teach young children something important. If you can, use a computer to word-process a neat script.

Save your script on disk so that you can easily change and improve it. You could go on to plan a performance and design a simple puppet theatre. Hanging your puppet up when it is not being used will stop the strings from tangling. Puppets have been made for a very long time and in many different places. Use a CD ROM and books to find out more about the world of puppets.

Moulded containers
Designing practical packages

Among the moulded products you see every day are many different bottles and containers. Shower gels, shampoos, deodorants, perfumes, aftershave, make-up and toothpaste all come in moulded packages. Designers often use models to try out their ideas and to avoid expensive mistakes. Containers don't just have to hold a product. They usually have to make people want to buy it, and give information. They should also be easy to use. Designers need to think about all the energy and materials that go into containers and what should happen to them when they are empty. How many moulded glass and plastic containers are there in your home? You don't have the machines to make plastic and glass containers but you can design and model them.

Safety: some liquids used in the home can be harmful. Get adult advice and make sure that containers you look at or take parts from are washed out thoroughly first.

You will need

- Plasticine
- air-drying clay or salt dough (page 7)
- paper
- colouring equipment
- bottle caps

What to do

1. Think about the design of your container and what would go in it if it was real. Read these two pages and draw different ideas before you start making (see page 10).

2. Start by making a basic shape and mould your container from that. A few examples are shown here. You could try out your ideas in Plasticine first because it won't dry out while you experiment.

3. To make your project look more real you could add a lid, cap or other part that you have found. Make a shape to hold it in place when you glue it.

4. Use fingers, modelling tools or a plastic knife to make the shapes you want. Cut-out shapes can be stuck on after brushing them with water.

5. Let your model dry if it is air-drying clay. Get adult help to bake a salt dough model and let it cool (see page 7).

6. Paint your model. If you want a shiny look, brush it with a water and white glue mixture.

7. Design a label for the front of your container. You could design one for the back as well. Look at real labels to get ideas.

Getting ideas

What would your container hold? It could be something to use in the shower, bathroom or kitchen, or somewhere else. Could it hold a special potion or magic medicine? Perhaps it will be home for a genie! Does the user have hobbies that give you ideas? Look at containers in your home as a starting point – but don't just copy them. What do you like about them and what do you dislike? Are they easy to use? Do they fit your hand? Think about how your container might be used. Will it be opened and used with wet or soapy hands? Will it stand on a shelf or hang on a hook? Could we re-use or re-cycle more containers? Think of new uses for used containers. Could yours be designed to have other uses?

Look at labels. Yours could have information, warnings, bar codes, ingredients and pictures. How will your labels and container make people want to buy the product? If you can, use a computer for very realistic labels.

Decorating people with mouldings
Making some jewellery

People have been wearing decorations for thousands of years. Some decorations tell us things, perhaps that someone is married. Other decorations show that the wearer has certain beliefs or that they belong to a club or other group. People have used almost every material to decorate themselves, including wood, feathers, animal teeth and shells. Jewels, gold, silver and other metals are often used as decoration. Metals are sometimes melted and poured into moulds to make jewellery. This is called casting (see page 18).

You can shape some mouldable materials to make decorations. Remember that decoration has to be practical too. Make sure that yours are not too heavy or fragile. It is very important that decorations are safe and comfortable as well as beautiful.

Safety

Use thin cotton to make sure anything hung round the neck or other part of the body *breaks easily* in case it snags on something.

You will need

- papier mâché pulp (page 8)
- drinking straws
- air-drying clay (page 7)
- foam plastic sheet (page 8)
- paints, thread and cotton
- other materials that you want to add

Medals, badges, brooches and pendants

1. Cut out shapes in clay or dough. Stick on any shapes with water and do any moulding. Add a safety pin or make a hole for hanging.

2. Paint your projects when the dough is baked or the clay is dry. Varnish with watered down white glue if you want a shiny finish.

Beads

1. Roll out a slab of salt dough or air-drying clay and cut or stamp out the shapes you want. Make holes with a cocktail stick for threading.

2. To make beads the same size, cut equal pieces from a cylinder. Mould the shapes and make holes. Lightweight beads can also be made by flattening some papier mâché pulp and folding it round a piece of straw.

Bracelets and bangles

1. Overlap and tape a circle of thin card so that it will slip on to your wrist.

2. Use a plastic bottle full of water to hold the circle while you add layers of papier mâché pulp. You could also try making a Mod-roc bangle (see page 8).

You could stick on extra shapes and paint when dry.

Bangles, bracelets and other decorations can be moulded from foam plastic sheet (see page 8).

1. Get adult help to warm the sheet in an electric oven.

2. Mould the sheet round something that is the right size and shape for your project.

Spirals can be made by winding strips of foam round a pencil or stick.

Join different colours by pressing pieces together under a board when they come out of the oven.

You can press things into the warm sheet to emboss it.

Getting ideas

Your decoration could be for a special theme party. You could design a matching set of fun jewellery. You might need to use colours that go with clothes or a costume. Look out for feathers, silk flowers, sequins, shells, small bells and other things to use with your mouldable materials. Could you add things to make a rattling or some other noise as the wearer moves? Beads can be worn round different parts of the body or sewn or tied on to fabric. Try cutting up extruded shapes (see page 16) to make beads. Could you invent an award and make a medal for it? You could use a computer to make a certificate too. You could design decoration that plays a part in a story or play. It might be very valuable or have special powers. Choose a lightweight material like papier mâché for large decorations. Look at other pages in this book for more methods you could use. For very large pieces look at page 20. To help with your own designs, find out about decoration and jewellery in different parts of the world and through history.

Moulding more things to eat

Food products such as chocolate, pastry and marzipan are mouldable. Ice lollies and fruit jellies are cast in moulds. Special cakes can be beautifully decorated by extruding icing through different-shaped nozzles. Biscuits are fun foods that can be made from mouldable materials. Bread dough is also easy to mould into many different shapes. Bread is an important food in many different cultures. Take a close look at different breads like granary, herb, malt, crusty, naan, pitta and rye. If you can get some to try, describe what they smell and taste like. Look in baker's shops, supermarkets and books to find out about new and traditional biscuits and breads. **Important**: Anything that will touch food must be really clean. Read about food safety and hygiene on page 9. Get adult help when using a hot oven.

You will need

- basic biscuit mix (page 9)
- 100g of icing sugar
- small sweets, dried fruit, other edible decorations
- basic bread mix (page 9)
- herbs, seeds and spices
- cocktail sticks, coloured paper, other things for decoration

Biscuits

1. Design your biscuits. Read these pages for help.

2. Use the basic mix or add flavouring to it. Ideas for different flavours include grated lemon or orange peel (wash the fruit first), grated chocolate, dried fruit and other safe flavourings. Ask adult advice and do not add too much. **Remember** that some people are allergic to nuts and other foods.

3. Cut or stamp out the shapes you want. Cutting gives you more choice. Try out shapes on paper and make a template. This is especially useful when you want lots of shapes the same.

4. Bake the biscuits (see page 9).

5. If you want to add icing, mix 100g of icing sugar with 1 tablespoon of warm water.

6. Spread the icing with a knife and press in sweets and other decorations. You can also draw and write on the biscuits using an icing syringe.

Bread

1. Design your bread project. Read these pages for help.

2. Use the basic recipe to make dough. Before adding water, mix in herbs and spices if you want them.

3. Make the shapes you want. Dough can be moulded and stuck together with water. Use a garlic press to extrude hair shapes (see page 16). Seeds and other things can be sprinkled on. Brushing your design with egg white will make it shiny when baked.

4. Bake (see page 9) and leave to cool well before tasting. Hot bread can burn!

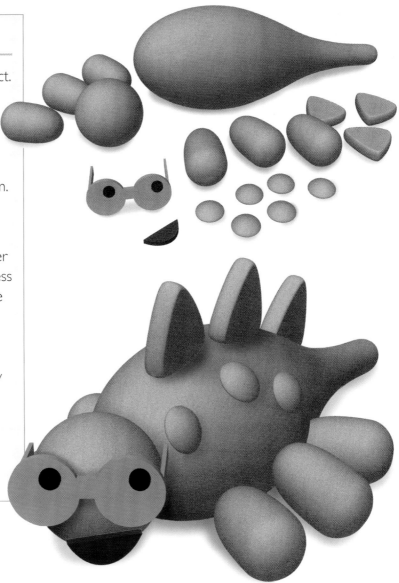

Getting ideas

How would you decorate your biscuits to show what flavour they are? Make up interesting names for them. You could make biscuits into a gift for someone.

Design a package that will protect the biscuits and look attractive. You could think about bags, boxes, packets, tubes and other ideas. Think of different ways to decorate your package and tell people about what is inside. Perhaps you could use computer graphics and word-processing. Collect pieces of ribbon and other attractive things for decoration. Collect and look at different biscuit packages.

Think about ways to flavour your bread. Will it be for a special party or picnic? Decorations could be added, like cocktail sticks and paper sails to make bread boats. Use a computer to print paper decorations that tell people about your bread or sandwich. You could design sandwiches with unusual but tasty fillings.

Grids for drawing

Square grid (see page 10)

Top of grid

Index